when he leaves
and other poems

Juliet K. Buesing

Copyright © 2018 Juliet Buesing

All rights reserved.

ISBN: 978-1979541978

For Rayyan, Bongi, Kasia, and Laura,
the friends who call anyway.

PROLOGUE

for the poets who feel

we were a lone
cry
in the night sky
our voices a giant knife
glinting silver in the starlight
threatening to rip open the heavens
and beat them empty
of their claim on
truth.

we were wretched,
writhing in our anxieties,
scrawling poetry into the places on our wrists
that would peel back the pain.

it did not heal us.
they still could not feel
the depths of our souls.
to know such an ocean of suffering
would be inhuman.
we were supernatural,
simultaneously living and
drowning,
egotistically insistent our blind stumbling a perfect path
of our own design.

we were our own drunken deities,
morally absolute and absolutely repugnant
baptizing ourselves in the spit from our own throats
cleansing our egos in backwash.

we begged to be loved,
let our favorite words
make out with each other,
whispered our souls like
they were
secret late-night affairs,
the scent of stale perfume
dogging us in the daylight.
we stretched our limbs to breaking
between poetry and sanity,
haunted by our own doubts
and demons
as we shook the
reverie from our eye lashes.

we were double agents-
for rational life on one hand
and truth on the other.
the nights were long.
the days were hard.

this is poetry? i asked him one day,
suddenly wishing for things to be simple,
easy...
and he said yes,
yes, this is poetry:

>	to be irreparably human and
>	to fail at love and life
>	to restlessly unsettle your heart
>	to be desperate for
>	things you do not know~

      to feel:
      to understand the language
      of your very aching bones
      the cries of creaking stardust
      still wishing for
      a better life,
      and the growing pains
      of a long battered and
      swollen
      universe.
      such is the burden of a poet.

and I felt the stardust,
the groans of my bones,
the futility of skyscrapers,
and breathed in
the inevitable death
of my own begotten darkness,
the dust I would become
and in fact
already was.

then,
at last,
i became a poet.

PART ONE
GRIEF

too soon

I have tried to write
a thousand poems
about it
but the hurt
cuts too deep, past the place
where words no longer go
where voices
cannot sing

-*not ready to talk yet*

moving, in three parts

i. betrayal/leaving

this house
has been mother to me
held me
when the shivering moon tugged too strong
and tide swept
road away, she
was boat
was anchor
could float me to sleep
with her wind-whispered lullabies.

ii. list/home

walked these floors like the wood
could feel the tender longing of my toes,
gently rinsed sunshine from dishes,
wiped heartbreak from windows
met dawn face-to-face
know each crevice
know how the walls whisper
why the tub leaks
know where the draft comes in
beneath the cupboards.

iii. empty/boxes

the problem with saying goodbye
to a home
is that there is no way
to say thank you
to a womb.

mountains

From the sky
the Rocky Mountains make me
think of crumpled paper,
wrinkled sheets on an unmade bed
beneath a faded
late morning sunshine,
or sometimes the raw edges
of scars on skin.

Mountains are the history of earth's violence
upon itself-
a territorial warfare
waged within the earth's core,
the painful adolescence of a planet in process,
or maybe the lovemaking of land itself;
the paths they trace across the continents are faint sketches
of a time that only God and plankton can remember.

They are also reminders of human insignificance:
there are still some places in the world
where the walls
and barriers
that bind and separate us
were not built
by mortal hands.

fill-in-the-blank

They tell me the
man in the sky
has a plan
and this is why
_____.

god-forsaken

The sky leans down
pregnant with murder,
swallows the air from the city,
wraps death's long, cold fingers around walls,

tightens into suffocated fists
snaps stones into rubble,
breathes death into dust
at the door frames of long-shuttered shops.

Deep in the belly
of the fury of the clouds
grief unwinds its piercing scream,
an echo whipped away in the wind,

sews itself back inside the emptiness,
sinks into deadened pain,
broods over the haunted silence.
A vengeant stillness reigns.

Here the sun weeps
over children's eyes and women's shoulders
for the life it will no longer give:
its daughters long disowned by hope,
its sons disinherited.

Even gods would pray
not to live through such days.

- for Aleppo

communion prayer

Heavy with unspun dreams
we prepare our hearts
for the dark ages looming
when ignorance and falsehood
may at last come to serve tyranny
over truth.

a dusk sets on our dreams, and we fear
to look too far into our future: for
the darkness is brutal, creeping, full of grief.

but today, we still live,
and we remember the joy of sunshine,
we delight in small things,
the laughter of our nieces and nephews:

for even if all is destroyed
but our very
descendants,
at least the children
will have been loved;
and love is a hatched seed
that takes root and
whose branches seek skyward
blossoming
for generations.

*- for the millennial generation, which
has grown up under threat of terrorism
and nuclear war, economic recession and
wage stagnation, climate change and other despairs*

when I try to explain what "racist" means

Like *sinner*
a word you say
on Sunday mornings
to ready yourself for redemption,
to break your heart into
impossible compassion
as communion bread would be,

Like confession: to be
a good person, you only have to
grieve and know that you, too,
are complicit
in a system of implicit biases,
like all of us: blind to our blindnesses,
living out legacies from a history we pretend
was bootstrap-built.

Like communal grief,
the sorrow and remorse
we share with
strangers.

Racist. It
was never an accusation,
only a prayer.

~ *we need a language to talk about this*

the murder on 4th street

There is something
Sighing in the
city this morning
amongst the lonely
orange barricades and
leering news cameras: a
broken spirit, sorrow,
agony
for a woman who
will not wake up,
collective grief for the
devils of terror
we have seen,
oddly familiar faces
lit beneath the torches' gleam.
Hate
makes fear out of
Home.

There is a breeze whispering between the bricks
this evening
on Fourth street. It carries away
last night's storm,
and all that happened here,
but the memory,
and the grief.

-for Charlottesville

school series

i. grownups

We heap adulthood on the shoulders of children,
more desperate that they know
how to survive our hell
than how to build
something divine
to replace it.

ii. starfish

First it is the art classes that disappear,
then the extra janitor,
then a few after-school buses.

The new set of books is delayed a year,
a sports team gets cut,
and the copy paper starts to dwindle;
then the rest of the after school-program vanishes,
and your two favorite teachers.

Then only half of a nurse is assigned,
and the library is closed;
the building is dustier, dirtier, and
there are only two administrators left,
drowning in paperwork
–they are all drowning in paperwork–
broken latches on windows,
leaking ceilings,
book bindings crusting off, heaters broken, laptops dead,
hallways unsupervised, classes understaffed,
children bored, anxious, unseen.
Perfectly meet-able needs left unmet.
The haggard looks on adults' faces.

There are too many children
and only a few of us left to
carry them.

You cannot save them all, he said of the starfish.
He gave no moral guidance for when starfish
are not starfish at all but children.
He kept silent on that subject.

When the good Samaritan came by
there was only one bleeding man on the side of the road.
But what was he supposed to do if there were hundreds?
Jesus didn't answer all of my unasked questions.

It is one thing when you live in a world where you are
asked for only one good deed, one neighborly act.

It is another thing entirely when you live in a world where
crisis is a norm, where children are unwanted, where children are caretakers, where children are desperate, where children are hurting, where children have only ever fallen
through the cracks.

Are children our neighbors?
What am I to do with all the starfish?
I haven't got enough hands.
I haven't got enough heart.

iii. teaching

It was my first love
but it nearly broke me.
So I left.

-for my students, who deserved the world

for Huma

For public shaming
and for sorrow
and the fear it could happen to us

and for the smart, beautiful women
who pay
when the men they love
do not get help for problems
they are sure they do not have.

For the handsome men
~such charmers!~
who beg us to bat our eyes at them
lest the tree that falls in the forest
would cease to exist, unseen and
unheard.

For the sadnesses we carry
that aren't even ours
once the gossip has run out
the laughter of ridicule run dry
and only the familiar, dry, cracked bed
of someone's pain
is left.

~ it was never funny

relationships summary

On the whole
they have a tendency
to think I am pretty, kind,
and a little too smart,
To suggest plans that
are not promises
(and thus do not come to pass),
To build unbelievably beautiful worlds
with their words,
unwittingly tempt me
with my own
dreams, and tie up
my hopes
in shackled ribbon.
I do not doubt
they honestly want
me to be happy.

But at the end of the day,
I am still alone on the couch,
watching *Friends*
for whatever
reason.

And I have learned
that there are plenty
of reasons.

Study of Beauty, Part II (spoken word)
Written as part of Not Dalton's Kids, a project by Alysia Harris

I've stolen
glances at you
among other misdemeanors.
All of you, us, we, women.
It seems I cannot decide if I want to protect you
in your weakness or envy you
in your weakness,
so I've resorted to a harmless pickpocketing,
nabbing the curves from your body,
the slimness off your arms,
the perfect architecture of your derriere-
I've stolen the salt from your eyes
and suckled the beauty off your lips
till you too
taste this silence- forgive me.
I am too strong to be a woman
and we are all too something to be beautiful.

Growing up was
our mothers teaching us how to do our hair;
separate like Sunday mornings,
we shed blood to prove we could break water,
and then we were told to walk onto the waves~
If God's son could do the impossible, what of his daughters
speaking forth their own Genesis?
let
there
be...
let there be cheap, harsh, fluorescent light
under which we are to shave and to wax and to
tweeze and to twist, to braid and to comb,
to iron and to cut and to dye,
we are dying,
losing our bodies to save our asses
lest no man declare us worthy of being watched,

for besides pain in childbirth,
this must be women's lot in life,
our beauty held hostage by the beholder.

I am not my hair
but mom always said that my hair betrayed
my free spirit: the hairdresser saw it was good,
but it didn't always do what it was told,
and it took me years to wake up on a Friday
and realize that beauty was on the other side
of cutting it off.

On some Saturdays I let the powder aside
in whose dishonesty we all are complicit
and I find myself at the mirror out of curiosity,
as if the mirror itself had forgotten
to reflect me,
as if it had forgotten who
I am, so I reach into the glass
and start painting myself like Vermeer
and I think his clouds have more grey
but I too see pinks and greens and golds
in between the browns of my white skin.

I didn't always think I was beautiful,
for beauty is not quite white,
but it is not quite brown or Black or Asian
or Latina or Native or mixed or you either,
and your beauty is a demon to my breasts,
and my beauty a devil to your hair,
and her beauty a pain in my ass...

So I dip my brush into every stolen glance,
and I'm painting us again
with all these pickpocketed goods,
and when I am done with the canvases
of our skins, our bodies,
our hairs,

my graffiti will paint itself onto the walls,
it will bleed out where our stilettos stab the floor,
and it will say in every color for every people that
I found Beauty
and she was in truth
and she was in our naked, just-washed bodies,
in the hair on our arms and the weariness under our eyes,
in our hips and our thighs and the breasts upon which our
babies might someday lay.

Beauty was in the eyes of the beheld:
and the Lord said that the eyes of a woman
is the lamp unto her soul,
for what she sees will fill her whole body with light
and make her shine—

So the graffiti I tag will be a great red arrow
twisting around the naked body of Eve,
streaking across her cheeks and pointing at her eyes, saying:
START here by looking to those windows of her soul—
precious souls of black onyx and gold and the very brown earth
and green-blue oceantide,
and the beautiful bodies that have been our homes
for all our lives—
Do you not find us beautiful at least for us that?
that this body is wondrously and fearfully mine?
Do you not love, as I do, the legs with which
I run to you, the hands with which I write to you,
the arms with which I hold you, the place
where I sit and the toes onto which I rise,
the hair that crowns me queen, the lips
from which my words burst forth,
the eyes through which I see?

And what woman
doesn't, honestly,
have stunningly beautiful eyes?

PART TWO
HOPE

monday

You ask me what I like about you
like you are confused,
like you have no idea what a treat it is
to see you smile.

work

You tell me
it is good for us
to miss each other.

I do not say
that 8 hours of such agony
is quite long enough.

I simply
invite you to lunch.

definition

Romance: arsonist
alighting hope,

melting
me into you,

recklessly,

I drain through
cracks
like water,

scatter
like ashes,

shatter
like windows
in a fire.

lover

Burrow your body
make your home in me
let's be together here~
Between the sheets.

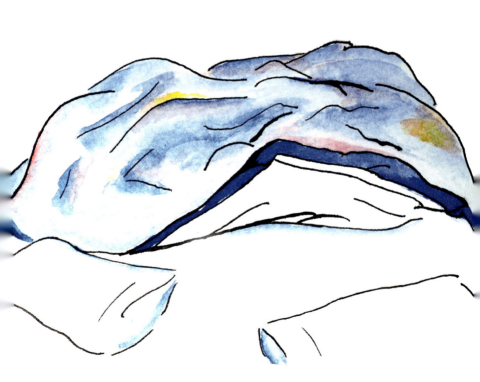

untitled

I never wanted
children
'til I met you.

VOWS

We will wrinkle
and grey
together.
Bury each other
and still stay
together.
Black tie funeral dates
together.

joy

I feel silly
all day
dreaming
of you.

the ex

I am not afraid
you would go back
to her. I am
afraid
she will take
my wide-eyed joy
and make it yet another
half-love
I talk myself into,
swallowing where it hurts
to keep you
from the pain
I feel
alone
where you don't see.

she was the one

who got away.
expert escape artist.
Your heart, however,
never got untied,
drowned in the ghosts
of her limbs.

grace

I have known saints
who catch my tears,
as precious pearls born
of salt-soaked lids;

hold me
on wretched nights
when my heart has ballooned
two sizes too big,
and shattered;

piece me together over
and over again
with the balm of their breath

let me run off to break
once more and
still
never give up

making me whole.

~ friends

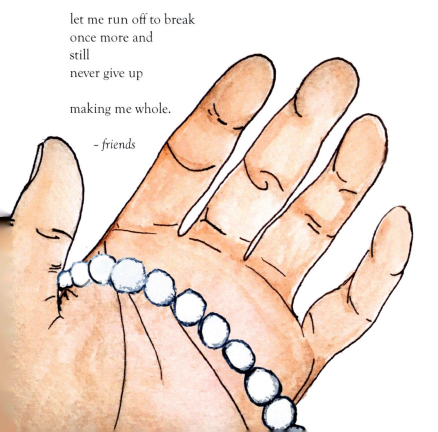

what the Earth said to the Sun

You are
a lot.
But maybe
you are the
a lot
that I want in my life,
the Earth said
to the Sun,
when before the stars
they swore
'til death do them part.

(Though in planetary cases,
death is a black hole, and
black holes really
prefer to keep things
together.)

it will never be a thing

The todayness of it
killed me,
freed him~
otherwise, our pillowtalk
could make the storm clouds jealous,
and our kisses could teach
the rain.

daydream

It is a cool Sunday afternoon,
grey, quiet,
a single lamp on.
in a daydream my lips
hover near your breath, warm,
heart flitting, fearful of touch
awaited too long, my arms
encircle, make bed of your
broad and burdened
shoulders. As you
pull me in close with tender and
wordless tongue, I feel
your palms build
a galaxy of goosebumps
on the small of my back. You

do not want me. Perhaps

you simply like having
options. I wonder if
you are still too young to know
what you want, or how
to make such worn and lonesome
decisions
as love.

Since you are far,
it is easier. I push it
away
and return to my book,
a less brutal kind of fiction.

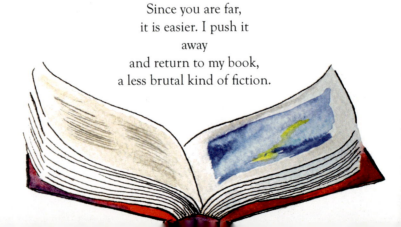

how it ended

He asked me to go
silently
between the laughter
and blue-skied
afternoons,
the sweet salt
of his tongue on mine.

He begged me
to leave,
wordlessly,
gently,
in the taut
stretch of his
shoulders,
the wary misery
in his eyes;

he told me
I wasn't
right
for him
any more.

So I left.

permission, or the hardest lesson

Believe it the first time
he makes you feel
small, unseen,
overlooked; the hour
he lets you weep
alone:
    No.

Listen to me: You are the sun,
the North Star, the naked autumn sky,
you are an earth-shattering comet,
the moon's diamond-studded frame.
You are wonder, grief,
passion, home.
What you touch feels loved
and seen— blessings drip from your fingertips.
You are beautiful, and ready,
the holiest, most terrifying truth.
You are a dream
walking on this earth.

If he does not know this
and hold onto you
with every tendon in his body,
love you
like your joy is his very air,
he is simply not the one.

Just leave, my love.
Leave.

sleepless

I do not doubt that time
heals many things,
that my heart,
bound and shaking,
will not always haunt
the wet corners
of my eyes, and
that there will be other
arms to enfold me,
other chests to burrow into.

But the night. Oh,
the devil's
dark whispering night.

the end

The taste of freedom
Bitter sweet your bones
Sucked marrow
From death to love me
For all the ways
I have loved you
Dry
For all the ways we have
Loved each other
Til sacrifice was the
Tendons from our broke bent
knees You said enough
was enough Forgave
me my shackles
And frail heart I wonder
if the silence
is a relief wonder if
Certainty will condemn
our demons to death
Wish love over you
from rains I no longer
will weep Wish against
my Sins
wish anything were
different
at all.

~ *for* K.

when he leaves

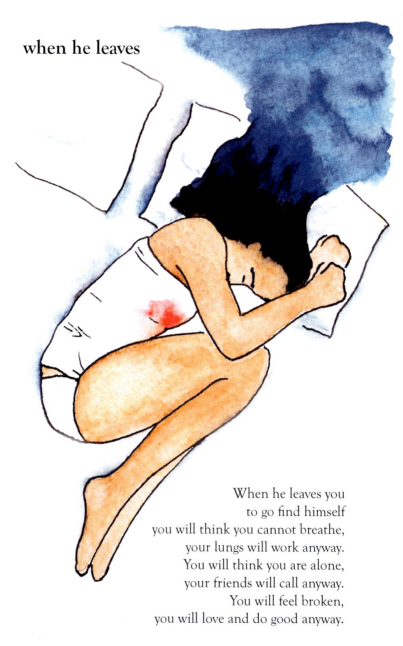

When he leaves you
to go find himself
you will think you cannot breathe,
your lungs will work anyway.
You will think you are alone,
your friends will call anyway.
You will feel broken,
you will love and do good anyway.

He was not the beginning
of your heart.
He will not be the end of it.

pleasantries

I would ask you
how you are
but I don't think
I can handle
the answer: if you
say you
are good I will know
it is because
she bathes between
the words that
slip over
your tongue.
If you
say you are hurting,
I might rip out
the very sky
over my soul
and coat you
in its sunshine
just to make you
feel whole.
Either way, I am
left shredded, asmoke,
my fragile and
glass-wrapped heart
invisible
to you still~ And
I am not ready
to become a
ghost, not ready
to be killed
by such
senseless
pleasantries.

advice

the last thing you want
is a man who is with you
because he doesn't want
to hurt your feelings
by leaving.

trust me baby sister,
you don't want to be
with a man
who doesn't want to be
with you.

so don't let him see your tears any more
take your space
breathe the air
turn your heart to other things.

let him go.

you can't always get what you want, love.
but everything will be okay.
someday soon there will be another.
there is always
another
for pretty catches
like you.

what I miss

I am not angry.
I am not broken.
I just miss you,
your hand
seeking mine whenever
we walked,
your forehead kisses
as you slipped into bed
with me, your
sense of humor
and your stories
and all the plans
we made
together.

timing

I do not blame you
for doing that
which hurt me. I am
only sad that the
world in its turning
could not time our
stars to better align~
but instead spun you off
into the dark
where I grope for
you in dreams
and find only
empty air.

heart-throb

It is in the stillness at the end of the day,
in the final breath before I get up
to get ready for bed,
that I feel my love for you
tugging with the weary weight of gravity
on my heart.
The hum of the refrigerator,
the sting of how I miss you,
and the single dim light of my living room,
seem to be the last constants
of the night.

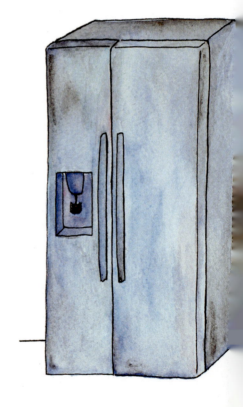

the human heart

Hearts are such strange and childish things.

To feel with such abandon
and to want so selfishly,
and to give so recklessly,
to fear loneliness~ or hurt,
or our own ability to hurt others~
so irrationally,
and all of this so compassionately:

how beautifully human we are.

promise

You must let
my heart break
for you
when you are in pain
without trying
to keep me from your hurt.
And
I must let you
be broken,
pick yourself up,
put the pieces back together
without trying to fix you.
This is what we agreed to
when we traded
slivers of our souls,
sewed them into each other's
heart strings,
that there will be nights like this forever
when I will cry for you,
and you will have to let me.

~ for B.

forgiveness

Dress me in water. Clean
my limbs and lips of
these memories. Start
again. Long before
our sins were spilled
against each other
and long after
the breaking has
turned to healing,
Let us start there,
in the middle of a love
full of grace no one else understands.

Easter, or nephew

In the breath of days
before belly
becomes person,
she pulls my hand to her side
and says Here, feel,
And all the promise
of a being her heart has already
sworn to love
more than herself,
without reason or charm,
voiceless and still unknown,
stretches and moves
beneath my palm.

It is Easter.
I wonder at the darkness he feels,
the nothingness he knows,
how he drops infinitesimally closer to the earth
with each step she takes,
her muscles readying his exit
into a world that awaits, wants,
loves him, too.

When we list the things raised to life
on sunny spring Sunday mornings,
we so often forget that
Mothers' bodies too roll away stones
from Easter tombs all their own,
Bring light from darkness,
Split land from sea.

I rest my hand gently on her belly,
And we wait
for him.

~ *For Dominic*

EPILOGUE

27

27 comes slowly
like a street sign I creep up to
in the traffic home from work.
27 seems terribly old to the 12-year-old inside my heart:
she was brave and bold
if a little too bullheaded for a world
that didn't end up always wanting to go her way.

27 is admitting that I
wasn't always honest
with myself,
was impatient,
didn't know the answers,
was wrong,
still needed help
I didn't know how to ask for.

27 is learning to grieve and love and lose and wonder
and be grateful all at once,
to be unable to answer simple questions
like "how are you?"
"what do you want?" or "why did you do that?"
or least of all:
"what does it mean?"

We are all from lost generations,
All six million years of us,
sweeping up dustpans full of narratives to cling to,
finding hope in clean dishes
and the joy of having someone to hold on to at night;
Even cavemen were afraid of the dark.

And we have all, for generations,
said we'd be in each other's corners,
but when the bell chimed,
found ourselves wearing bloodied gloves,
crouched in opposite ends of the ring,
still hoping to win:
27 is finding out that love can be selfish.

And 27 is learning that love can be a good bye,
That not all loves are permanent adhesive; some are more like
buffeting wind currents,
that there is a love that doesn't stick but sets free
gives up
moves on
burns out,
and this is not a failure,
even though it hurts,
and makes you cry.

And 27 is finding out that goodness can be small;
That surviving evolution, supervolcanoes, and meteorites
for 6 million years
is a tiny feat of human luck
that allows us to participate in tiny feats of human kindness
in return.

27 is a recipe book that is slowly filling up,
written in an ink of spilled memories you feel too young
to be etching with this much nostalgia.

27 is traveling the world
to find that all along
you just needed to call mom.

27 is a testament
to the friends whose names fill up
your calendars and your memories and your dinner table
and the other halves of your inside jokes.

27 is an obsolete insistence on paper books
in the age of Kindle.

27 is shoveling your own damn driveway,
doing your own damn laundry
cooking your own damn soup.

27 is recognizing that this world is not really your own
that there was no oyster.
It is knowing you might stop hoping and fighting tomorrow
if there were no children,
but there are children,
though they aren't your own.

27 is being pretty sure you are messing something up.
But since no one really knows the words to this song anyway,
it's turning up the volume,
and singing your heart out,
and moving your feet and hips
like this whole world of lonesome, frightened fools
should join in the joy
and dance to 27
too.

Or to whatever numbers they want, really.
The music is universal.

AKNOWLEDGMENTS

Thank you to Zachary Taylor and Rayyan Kamal for editing; to Jenn Shenk for artistic guidance; to Matt Davis for photography; to all the people in my life who inspired these poems and supported the creation of this book; to Courtney, John, and Bart for encouraging my poetry; to my students, especially Nick, Hibak, Dubem, and Rasheem, for inspiring me; and to you, for making my art and poetry a part of your life.

ABOUT THE AUTHOR

Juliet Buesing lives in Charlottesville, Virginia with her dog Coby (and lovely roommate Steph). In addition to writing poetry, singing jazz, and watching a lot of Arrested Development, she works as a literacy specialist in a local elementary school and attends the University of Virginia schools of Public Policy and Law. Previously, she was a high school English teacher in the Boston Public Schools and served as a slam poetry coach for the Louder than a Bomb state champion youth team, Urban Ego.

Made in the USA
Middletown, DE
11 March 2018